# THOMAS ROUSSET

# LE MANOIR AUX QUAT' SAISONS

OXFORDSHIRE

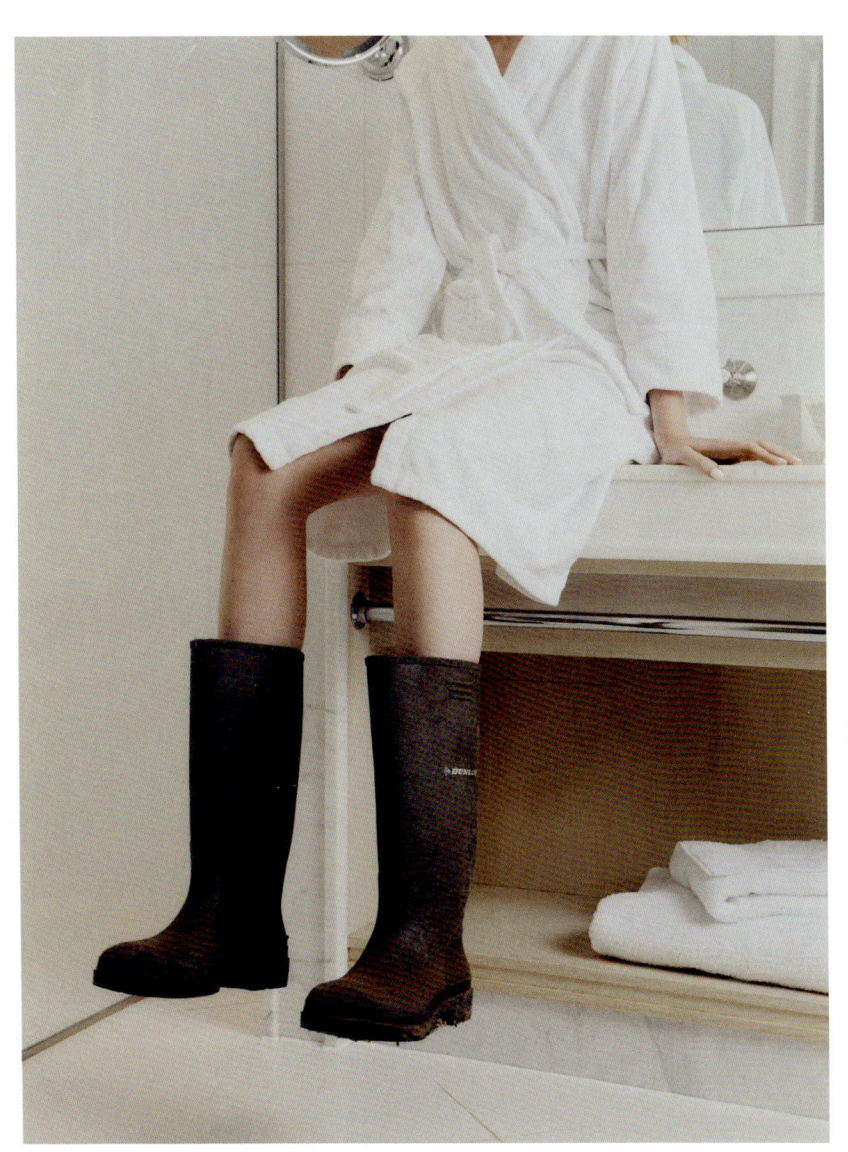

Thomas Rousset
Le Manoir aux Quat'Saisons

French photographer Thomas Rousset charaterises his distinctive style as 'magical photorealism', combining a documentary aesthetics with a surrealist narrative. This approach is exemplified in his major project *Prabérians* (2022), which depicts a fictional rural community based on the modest mountain village near Grenoble where he grew up. Drawing inspiration from the cinema of Emir Kusturica and Tim Burton, he transforms the town of Prabert into scenes imbued with a touch of the absurd. His work engages with the seemingly bizarre and random acts that punctuate the everyday, questioning the rituals and behaviours that have become commonplace in modern society.

Rousset's penchant for surrealism also informs his photographs of Le Manoir aux Quat'Saisons, a Belmond hotel in Oxfordshire, England. Renowned for its expert restoration of iconic properties, the luxury hotel group is now collaborating with a select group of photographers to create a series of photographic works that respond to the unique character of each hotel and its surroundings. Rousset's irreverent approach made him the perfect choice to showcase the extraordinary stories that lie behind this Belmond destination.

Rousset's images of this 15th-century manor house were inspired by two distinct sources. Firstly, he drew on his own imagination of the luxurious lifestyle of the English aristocracy. Secondly, he was influenced "by the unreal, fantastical aspect" of the countryside lifestyle as depicted in old British films. By placing ordinary objects and figures in bizarre, dreamlike contexts, he disrupts the viewers' sense of reality, prompting them to reflect on what they are seeing. His fairytale images are not simply a showcase for the amenities and aesthetics of the hotel; they tell a story, creating an intriguing visual narrative that encourages viewers to project themselves into these exquisite settings.

Set in the idyllic English countryside, Le Manoir is perhaps most renowned for its esteemed chef and founder Raymond Blanc, a seminal figure in gastronomy and a pioneer in the field of food ethics and sustainability. Thomas Rousset invited the staff at Le Manoir to collaborate with him in the creation of elaborately constructed tableaux that use humour to underline the innovative and playful nature of Blanc's cuisine, as well as highlighting the property's exceptional gardens.

In one photograph, a receptionist's head is obscured by a giant cabbage leaf; in others, delicate desserts are placed on lily pads, or a waiter carefully holds a plate of sweets at waist level in the grass. Through these images, Rousset presents a whimsical vision of the refined lifestyle of this hotel. Under his gaze, it takes on an enigmatic, even hypnotic quality, and seems to exist outside of time.

Thomas Rousset photographed Le Manoir aux Quat'Saisons, a Belmond Hotel in Oxfordshire, in summer 2023 and summer 2024.

Creative direction: Dani Matthews, 20xx

Text: Laurie Hurwitz

Cover design: Eliott Grunewald

Set Design: Staci Lee Hindley

Post-production: Solis Retouch and Studio RM

Printer: Grafiche Veneziane

Editorial coordination: Miléna Chevillard

Publisher: RVB Books, Matthieu Charon, Rémi Faucheux

Acknowledgements: Roberta Pinna, Ally Beasy and the special thanks to Federico Gioco, Federico Covarelli, Wynston Shannon, 20xx Agency; Philippe Simonet, Jael Rabitsch, Céline Roubaud, Lea Felices, Sephora Petitot, Valentin Loredo and Violette Van den Berg, François Larpin, Maddy Perkins, Philippine Vieubled and the team at Voodoo Pictures, Jessa Thorpe, Sophia Wilcox, Rhianon Taylor, Channatip Chanvipava & Sarah Pauley

A huge thank you to the Le Manoir aux Quat'Saisons' team for supporting and taking part in this project; Raymond Blanc, Luke Selby, Theo Selby, Nathanial Selby, Liam Skelton, Benoît Blin, Glen Sharman, Julia Sutcliffe, Amy Black, Kristin Fowler, Beyonce Willett, Chloe Milne, Clive Jones, Ellis Cook, Emma Dickson, India Hunt, Jade Walker, Jean Giraud, Jimmy Dore, John Driscoll, Martin Casey, Nadya Pearson, Sam Frederick Taylor, Simone Du Preez and Ruth Ligget

Lastly, a special thanks for the support and creative ambition of Arnaud Champenois and his team, in particular Blue Bushell, Elle Hodson and Jonathan Openshaw

© Belmond Management Limited and RVB Books, 2024
© Thomas Rousset for the photographs
© Laurie Hurwitz for the text
ISBN 978-2-492175-51-0
Achevé d'imprimer en septembre 2024 en Italie.
Dépôt légal septembre 2024.